Dinosaur Life Activity Book

by Donald Silver

Illustrated by Patricia Wynne

DOVER PUBLICATIONS, INC.

New York

TO HONOR TED RILEY

Dinosaur Life Activity Book is a new work, first published by Dover
Publications, Inc., in 1988.

International Standard Book Number
ISBN-13: 978-0-486-25809-6
ISBN-10: 0-486-25809-2

Manufactured in the United States by LSC Communications
25809216   2018
www.doverpublications.com

Alamosaurus

Tyrannosaurus rex

Alamosaurus

Everyone knows about dinosaurs, but no one has ever seen one. Dinosaurs lived
millions of years ago. Then they died out and were gone forever.

1

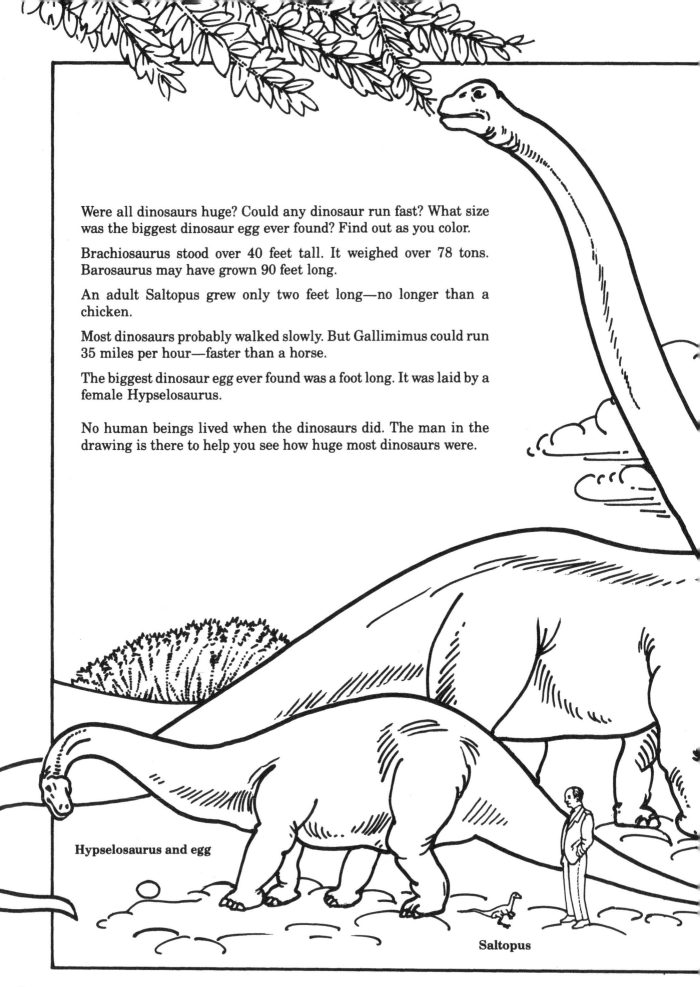

Were all dinosaurs huge? Could any dinosaur run fast? What size was the biggest dinosaur egg ever found? Find out as you color.

Brachiosaurus stood over 40 feet tall. It weighed over 78 tons. Barosaurus may have grown 90 feet long.

An adult Saltopus grew only two feet long—no longer than a chicken.

Most dinosaurs probably walked slowly. But Gallimimus could run 35 miles per hour—faster than a horse.

The biggest dinosaur egg ever found was a foot long. It was laid by a female Hypselosaurus.

No human beings lived when the dinosaurs did. The man in the drawing is there to help you see how huge most dinosaurs were.

Hypselosaurus and egg

Saltopus

Barosaurus

Brachiosaurus

Gallimimus

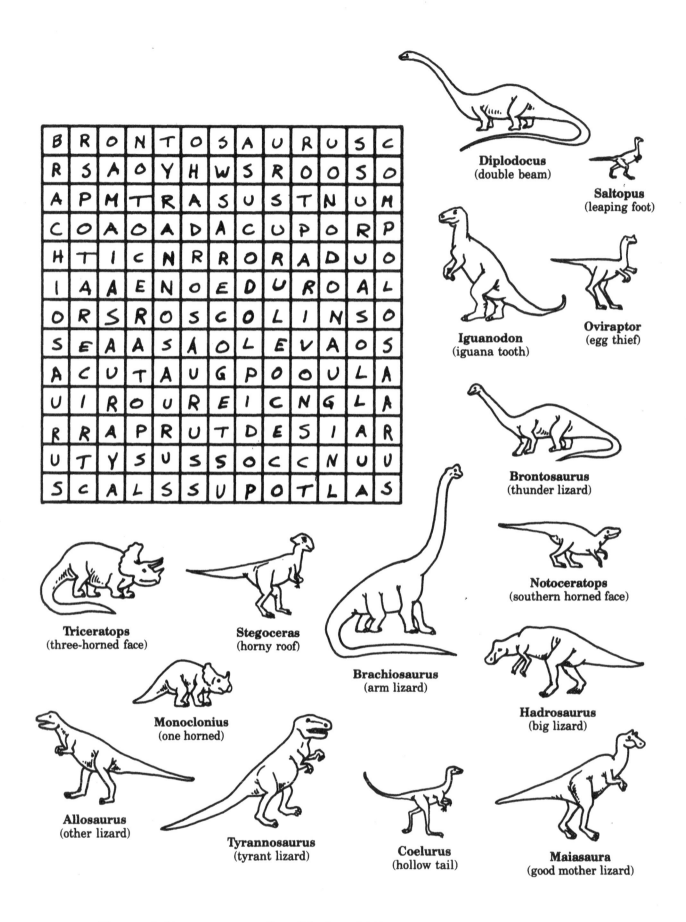

The word dinosaur means "terrible lizard." Each picture has the name of the dinosaur, with its meaning. Circle each name in the word box.

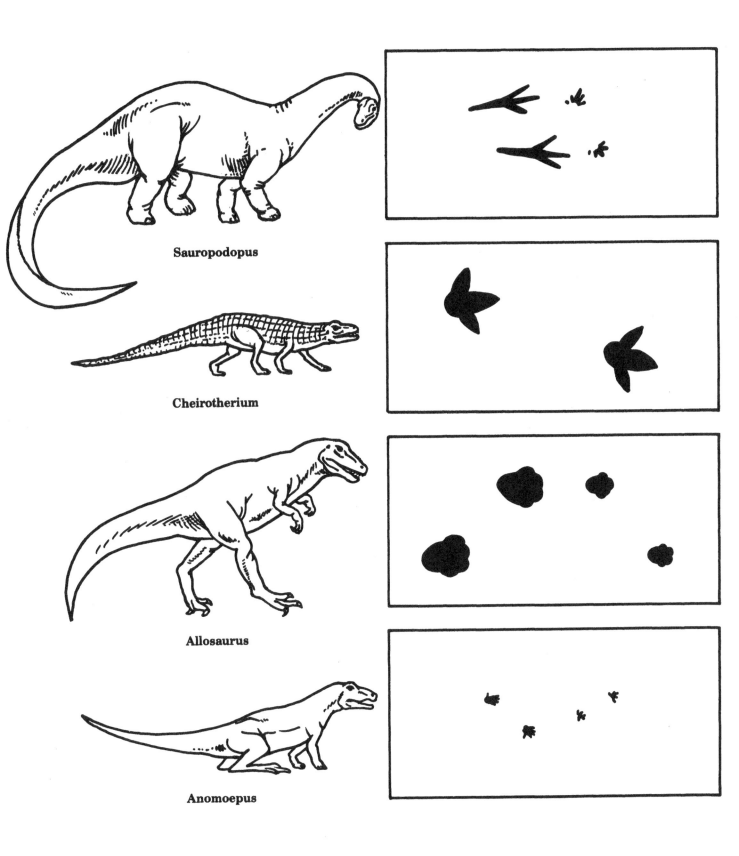

Sauropodopus

Cheirotherium

Allosaurus

Anomoepus

Fossils are remains of plants and animals that lived millions of years ago. We know about dinosaurs from fossils. People have found fossil dinosaur bones, teeth, skin, even footprints. Match the fossil footprints to the dinosaur that made them.

A dinosaur "hunter" is looking for fossils. Connect the dots and discover the fossil dinosaur bones hidden in the rocks.

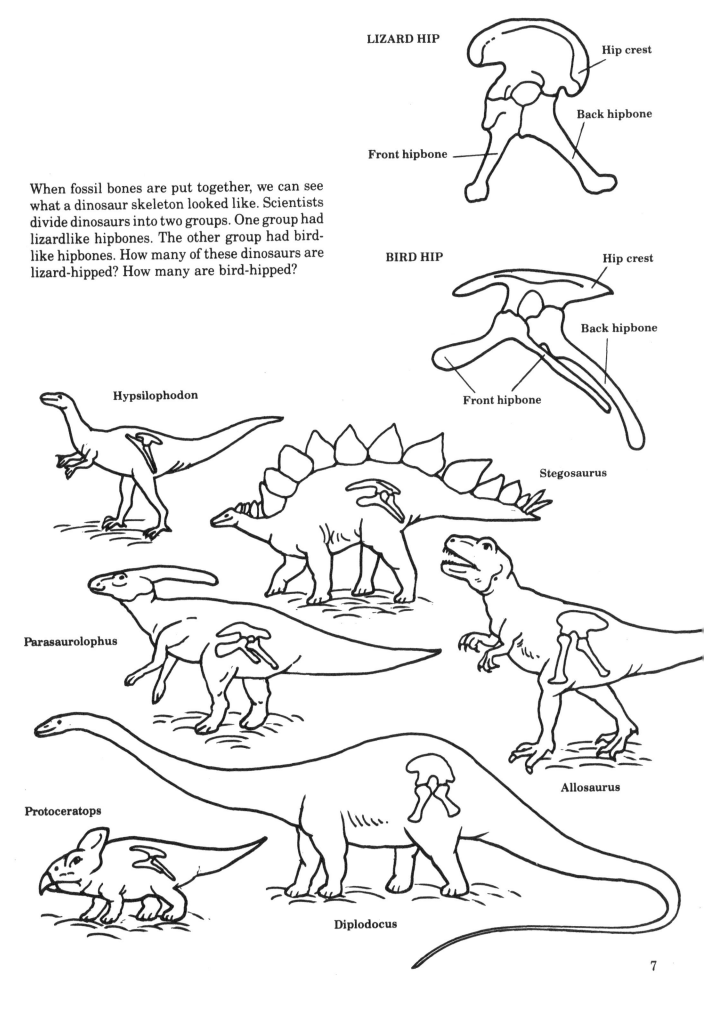

LIZARD HIP

Hip crest

Back hipbone

Front hipbone

When fossil bones are put together, we can see what a dinosaur skeleton looked like. Scientists divide dinosaurs into two groups. One group had lizardlike hipbones. The other group had bird-like hipbones. How many of these dinosaurs are lizard-hipped? How many are bird-hipped?

BIRD HIP

Hip crest

Back hipbone

Front hipbone

Hypsilophodon

Stegosaurus

Parasaurolophus

Allosaurus

Protoceratops

Diplodocus

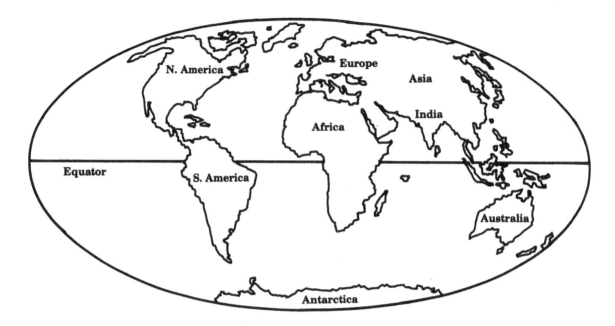

1. Earth is over 4.5 billion years old. This is a map of what earth looks like today. It has seven continents. But earth did not always look like this. For millions of years it has been changing.

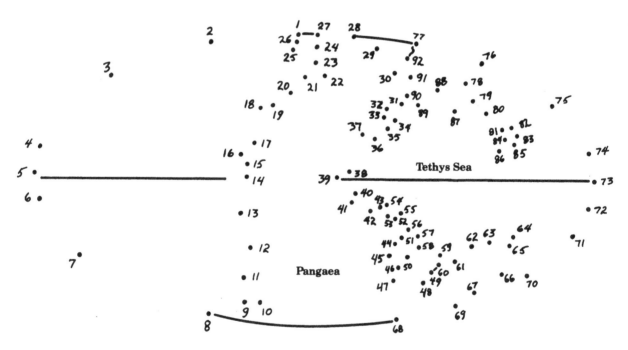

2. Dinosaurs lived during the Age of Reptiles. The Age is divided into three periods: the Triassic, the Jurassic and the Cretaceous. The first dinosaurs lived during the Triassic Period, which started about 225 million years ago and lasted about 35 million years. Connect the dots to find out what earth looked like at the start of the Triassic.

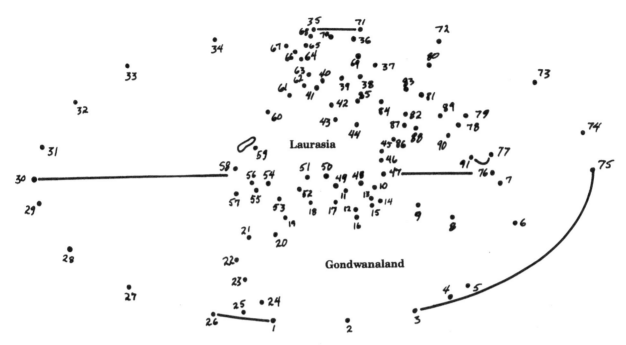

3. Because all the continents were joined together, dinosaurs could move every-where across the land. But during the late Triassic and the Jurassic Periods, the continents started to drift apart. The Jurassic Period lasted 54 million years. Connect the dots to find out how far the continents had drifted since the Triassic Period.

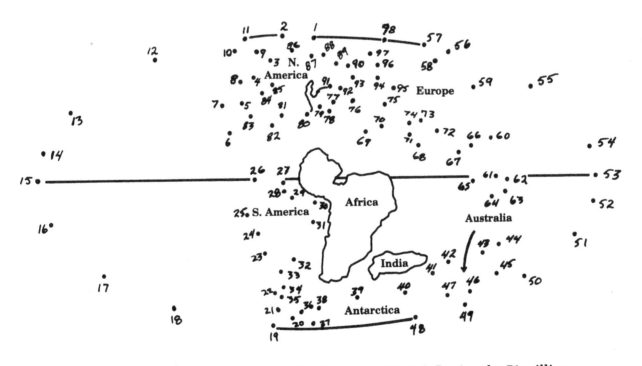

4. The last dinosaurs lived during the Cretaceous Period. During the 71 million years it lasted, the continents continued to separate. Connect the dots to find out which parts of the land were no longer joined together. They are marked with the names of the present continents and subcontinents into which they developed.

Plateosaurus

Color the Triassic.

The Triassic Period lasted from 225 million years ago to 190 million years ago. The climate on earth was warm and dry all year long. There were no flowering plants or grasses on the land where the first dinosaurs roamed.

Plateosaurus

Saltopus

Saltoposuchus

Four hungry Teratosauruses want to make a meal of the plant-eating Plateosaurus, but only one can make it to the center of the maze. Which one is it?

Most dinosaurs were peaceful plant-eaters. They had leaf-shaped teeth for chopping and mashing tough plant parts. Fierce meat-eating dinosaurs had long, sharp claws for attacking their prey. They sliced into their victims with their sharp, pointed fangs.

Fang

Leaf-shaped
tooth

13

Ten animals—dinosaurs and other Triassic reptiles—are hidden in this land-scape. Circle all of them.

14

Connect the dots to find out what a Coelophysis probably looked like. It was small, had a long neck and tail, walked on its hind legs and ran on its toes. Fossil Coelophysis bones have been found in New Mexico.

Rhamphorhynchus

Dimorphodon

By the end of the Triassic Period, there were flying reptiles called pterosaurs. The picture at the right looks like the one at the left, but it is different in six ways. Circle all the differences.

Protosuchus

Saltoposuchus

Coelophysis

During the late Triassic Period, some dinosaurs ate small lizards and croco-
dilians. Dinosaurs, pterosaurs and crocodiles were the ruling reptiles. They are
called Archosaurs. Circle the nine ways in which the picture on the bottom is
different from the picture on top.

Color the Jurassic.

The Jurassic Period was the second part of the Age of Reptiles. It lasted from 190 to 136 million years ago. Giant plant-eating and meat-eating dinosaurs roamed the warm earth. Flying reptiles fed on insects or fishes and the first birds took to the air.

Rhamphorhynchus

Allosaurus

Archaeopteryx

Coelurus

Stegosaurus

Apatosaurus
(Brontosaurus)

All of the fossil bones of the giant Brachiosaurus have been found. Just the shoulder bone is shown here. Brachiosaurus grew between 75 and 90 feet long. It could raise its head 40 feet above the ground. Connect the dots to find out if Brachiosaurus had a short neck or a long one.

Brachiosaurus

Only the fossil shoulder bones of the "Supersaurus" and the "Ultrasaurus" have been found. (Scientists have not yet decided what their real names will be.) Connect the dots to discover how much higher than Brachiosaurus these dinosaurs may have held their heads.

"Supersaurus"   "Ultrasaurus"

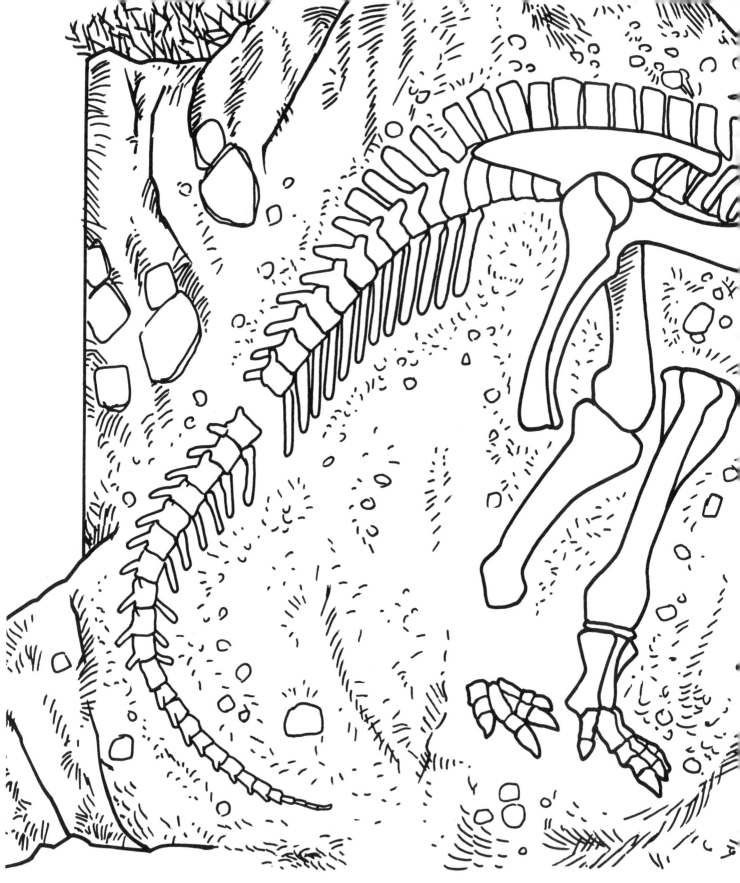

A paleontologist (fossil expert) has found some fossil bones. They belong to a Camptosaurus that lived about 140 million years ago. Help complete the skeleton by drawing a line from each of the six remaining fossils to the place on the skeleton where it belongs.

What's drinking at the stream? Connect the dots to reveal a Stegosaurus. The Stegosaurus had a row of stiff bony plates running along its back and sharp spikes on its tail.

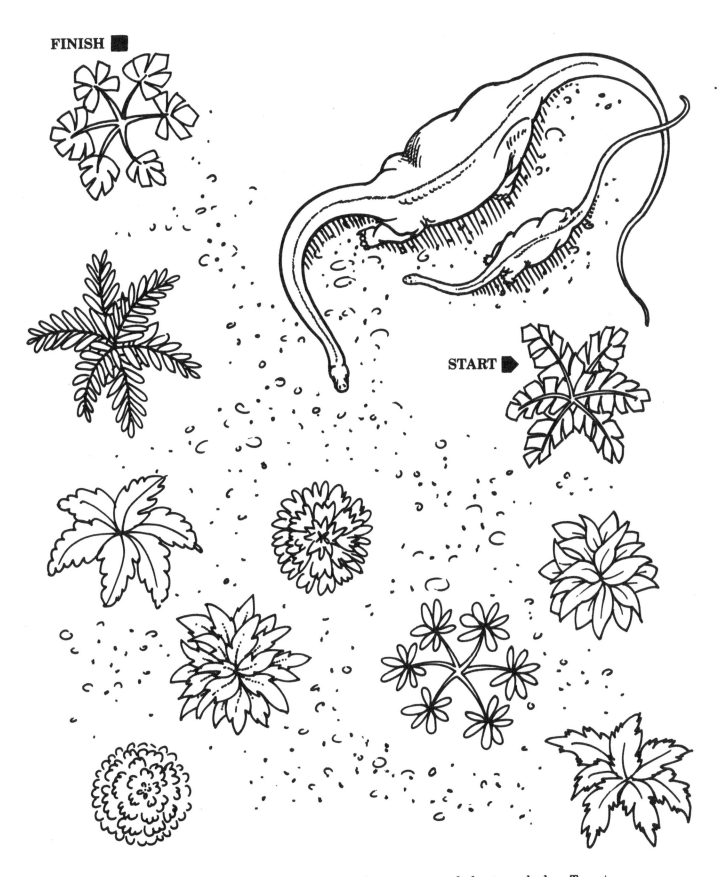

FINISH

START ▶

Some large plant-eating dinosaurs had to eat tons of plants each day. To get enough food, these Diplodocuses have to eat parts of each of these plants. But they can't visit the same plant twice. Using four straight lines, connect all the plants to show the dinosaurs how to visit each plant just once. Hint: None of the lines cross.

A giant Allosaurus is hunting a herd of Apatosauruses. Show it how to get through the maze. (Another name for Apatosaurus is Brontosaurus.)

START

FINISH

27

Tyrannosaurus rex

Color the Cretaceous.

Dinosaurs ruled the land during the Cretaceous Period, which lasted from 136 to 65 million years ago. Pterosaurs and birds flew above the dinosaurs. The warm climate on earth grew damp, and flowering plants multiplied. Crocodiles, tortoises, lizards and many small mammals increased in number.

Edmontosaurus

kylosaurus

Triceratops

Leptoceratops and young

29

U	L	R	A	S	I	T	O	P	E	M	C	D	B	V	N	K	Y
1	2	3	4	5	6	7	8	9	10	11	12	13	14	15	16	17	18

Use the code to spell the names of dinosaurs that lived during the Cretaceous Period.

1. _ _ _ _ _ _ _ _ _
   8 15 6 3 4 9 7 8 3

2. _ _ _ _ _ _ _ _ _ _ _ _
   12 4 11 9 7 8 5 4 1 3 1 5

3. _ _ _ _ _ _ _ _ _ _ _
   2 4 11 14 10 8 5 4 1 3 1 5

4. _ _ _ _ _ _ _
   7 3 8 8 13 8 16

5. _ _ _ _ _ _ _ _ _ _ _ _
   2 10 9 7 8 12 10 3 4 7 8 9 5

6. _ _ _ _ _ _ _ _ _ _ _ _
   4 16 17 18 2 8 5 4 1 3 1 5

1. Oviraptor   2. Camptosaurus   3. Lambeosaurus
4. Troödon   5. Leptoceratops   6. Ankylosaurus

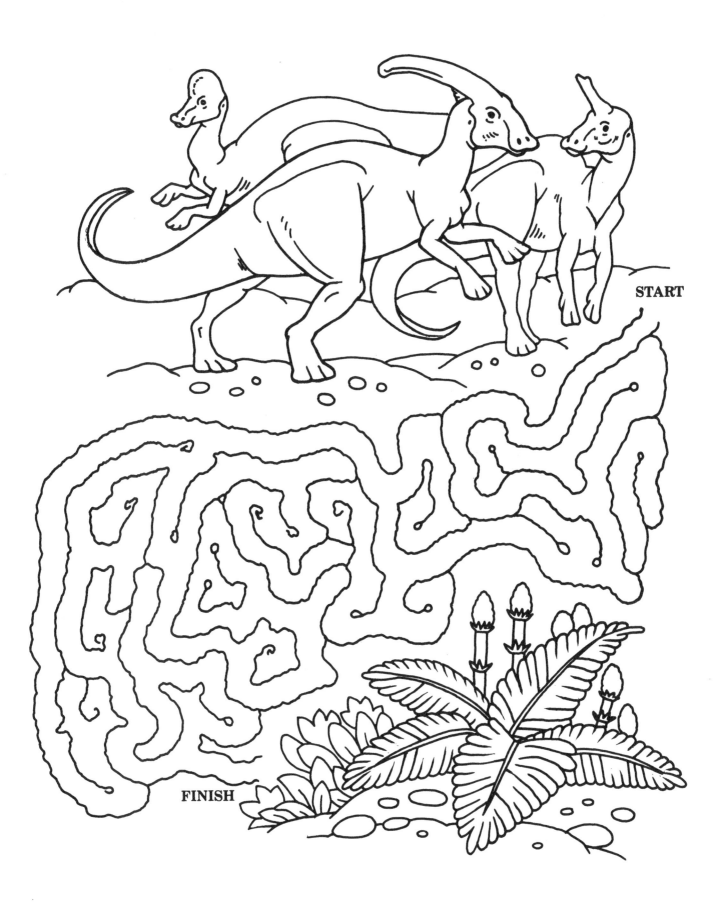

START

FINISH

Duckbill dinosaurs, or hadrosaurs, were peaceful plant-eaters. Many had bony head crests or special skin flaps. Help the hungry hadrosaurs reach the plants at the other end of the maze.

A herd of Triceratops senses danger and forms a circle. Each Triceratops stands ready to fight with its sharp horns. Triceratops grew 30 feet long and weighed about six tons. Connect the dots to find out what the Triceratops are protecting inside their circle.

Connect the dots and count how many Tyrannosauruses are closing in on the herd of Triceratops. Tyrannosaurus could grow 40 feet long and stand nearly 20 feet high. Sharp teeth lined a Tyrannosaurus' powerful jaws.

Color the Cretaceous Sea.

No dinosaurs lived in the sea. But during the Cretaceous Period long-necked plesiosaurs and 30-foot-long flippered mosasaurs ruled the seas.

Hesperornis

Archelon

Elasmosaurus

Ammonite

Belemnite

Tylosaurus

START

FINISH

A female Maiasaura laid her eggs in a nest. Then she covered them with sand to help keep them warm. Now her eggs are starting to hatch. Help the Maiasaura get through the maze to her nest before some other dinosaur eats her young.

Circle all eight dinosaurs hidden in this Cretaceous landscape.

Two male Stegocerases bang heads with each other. They are fighting to become leader of a herd of females. Circle the ten ways in which the picture on the bottom is different from the picture on top.

Unscramble the letters to spell the names of dinosaurs you have seen in this book.

SOTNURSBROAU (page 4)

1. __ __ __ __ __ __ __ __ __ __ __

GOSSSEURAUT (page 24)

APCRITTSORE (page 32)

2. __ __ __ __ __ __ __ __ __ __ __

3. __ __ __ __ __ __ __ __ __ __

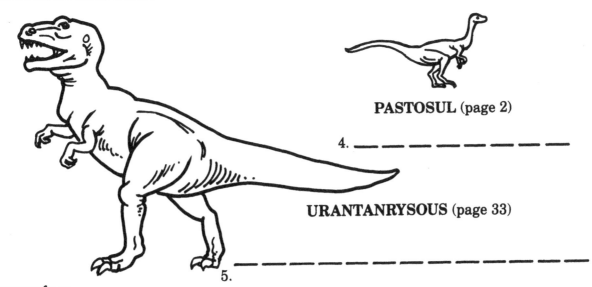

PASTOSUL (page 2)

4. __ __ __ __ __ __ __

URANTANRYSOUS (page 33)

5. __ __ __ __ __ __ __ __ __ __ __ __ __

SOLVE THE CROSSWORD PUZZLE.

Pteranodon

Stegosaurus

Across

1. _ _ _ _ _ _ _ _ _ means terrible lizard. (page 4)

4. Dinosaurs hatched from _ _ _ _ _. (page 36)

5. Triceratops had three _ _ _ _ _ _ on its head. (page 4)

7. The first dinosaurs lived during the _ _ _ _ _ _ _ _ _ Period. (page 10)

Down

1. Hadrosaurs were _ _ _ _ _ -billed dinosaurs. (page 31)

2. _ _ _ _ _ _ _ _ _ _ _ _ had a row of plates down its back. (page 24)

3. Dinosaurs lived during the Age of _ _ _ _ _ _ _ _ _. (page 8)

6. Some dinosaurs were _ _ _ _ _ -eaters. (page 12)

40

SOLUTIONS

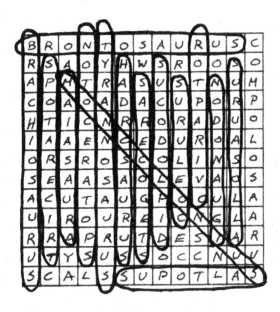

page 4

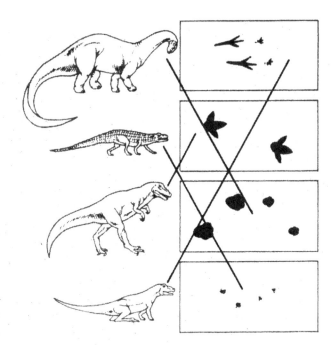

page 5

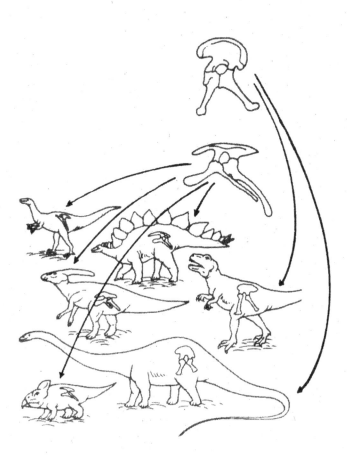

page 7

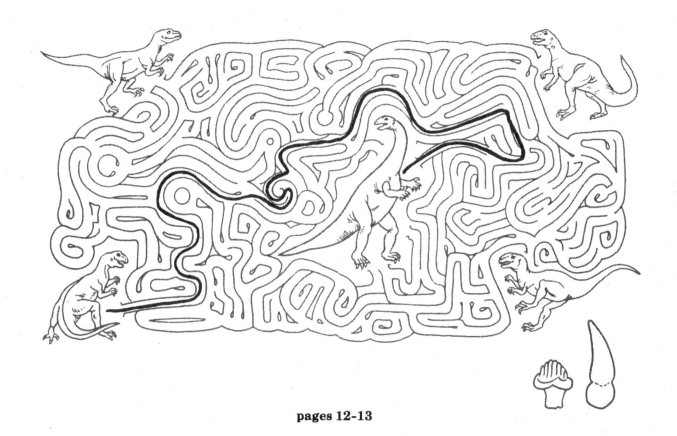

pages 12-13

page 14

page 16

page 17

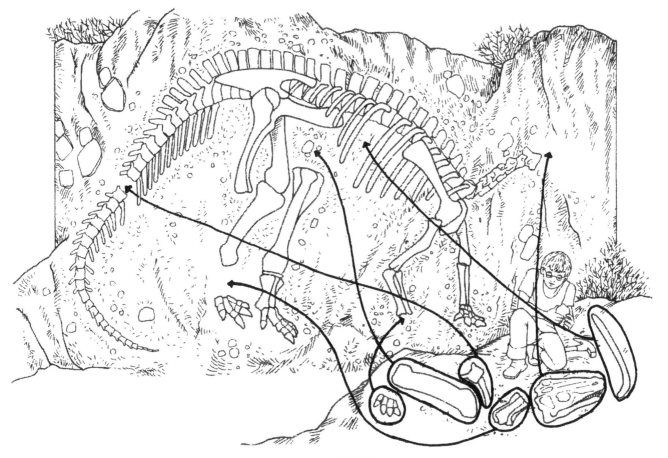

pages 22–23

page 25

pages 26–27